ULTIMATE TEDDY
B·E·A·R

THE LITTLE BOOK OF

TRADITIONAL BEARS

PAULINE COCKRILL

Introduction by Paul and Rosemary Volpp

Reader's Digest

The Reader's Digest Association (Canada) Ltd.
Montreal

A DORLING KINDERSLEY BOOK

PROJECT EDITOR Polly Boyd   ART EDITOR Vicki James
MANAGING EDITOR Mary-Clare Jerram   MANAGING ART EDITOR Gill Della Casa
PRODUCTION MANAGER Eunice Paterson

PUBLISHED IN CANADA IN 1992
BY THE READER'S DIGEST ASSOCIATION (CANADA) LTD.
215 REDFERN AVENUE, WESTMOUNT, QUEBEC H3Z 2V9

FIRST PUBLISHED IN GREAT BRITAIN IN 1992
BY DORLING KINDERSLEY LIMITED,
9 HENRIETTA STREET, LONDON WC2E 8PS
COPYRIGHT © 1992 DORLING KINDERSLEY LIMITED, LONDON

Canadian Cataloguing in Publication Data
Cockrill, Pauline
   The little bear library

Contents: [v. 1] The little book of bear care.– [v. 2] The little book of celebrity bears. –
[v. 3] The little book of traditional bears.
Each title also issued separately.
ISBN 0–88850–199–4 (set) – ISBN 0–88850–197–8 (v. 1) –
ISBN 0–88850–196–X (v. 2) – ISBN 0–88850–195–1 (v. 3)

   1. Teddy bears – History. 2. Teddy bears – History – Pictorial works. 3. Teddy bears –
Repairing. 4. Teddy bears – Collectors and collecting. 5. Teddy bears – Pictorial works.
I. Title. II. Title: The little book of bear care. III. Title: The little book of celebrity bears.
IV. Title: The little book of traditional bears.
NK8740.C63 1992   688.7'24   C92–090298–7

READER'S DIGEST and the Pegasus logo are registered trademarks of the
Reader's Digest Association, Inc.

Computer page make-up by The Cooling Brown Partnership, Great Britain
Text film output by The Right Type, Great Britain
Reproduced by Colourscan, Singapore
Printed in Hong Kong

92 93 94 95 96 / 5 4 3 2 1

❧ CONTENTS ❧

❧· INTRODUCTION ·❧

by Paul and Rosemary Volpp

In the late 1970s, British actor Peter Bull appeared
on numerous talk shows in Britain and the U.S. saying,
essentially, "Look! It's all right for grown-ups to like teddy
bears!" He received letters by the bucketful from adults who
had rather sheepishly kept their childhood bears packed away
for decades! This is how Peter Bull came to be called the
"father" of the current teddy bear craze.

———— ·❧· ————

Between the covers of this book you will
become acquainted with some wonderful
traditional bears. What makes a teddy bear
"traditional"? The dictionary defines the
word as "handed down by tradition:
conventional, customary."
Mathematical designs come to
mind as we think of the original
turn-of-the-century teddies. The
American Ideal bear is identifiable by
its triangular face. Most of the early
teddy bear manufacturers repeated
this feature to some degree. The
early British bears had more of
the solidity of a square –
they had rounded faces,
shorter noses, shorter

EARLY STEIFF
Bruno, a 1909 Steiff bear from
Paul and Rosemary Volpp's
collection in California.

1950S BEAR
*A teddy bear made by
Schuco in the 1950s in
the US zone of Germany.*

arms, larger thighs, and smaller feet. The early French bears we have seen were quite willowy – like French fashion models. They would fit into a narrow rectangular mold. German bears combined many angles. They still reflected Richard Steiff's love of the real bears he sketched so tirelessly at the Stuttgart zoo. They had longer limbs, larger feet, pointed muzzles, and the pronounced hump on the back.

• ❧.❧ •

This might be a good time to pass on a recognition tip we received from one of our earliest teachers. Study the features and shapes of teddy bears. Depend more on these features and shapes for identification purposes rather than nose stitching and the number of paw stitches. It is quite likely that the stitching has been redone at some point in time by a clever seamstress, either to make the teddy bear more attractive or more salable. And it is also possible that the stitching might have been changed to suit an owner's fancy. The body contours – the shape of the head, size of the feet and paws, and proportions of the limbs – are more likely to have remained unchanged.

KEY FEATURES
*A 1907 American bear displays
traditional features – long limbs,
large feet, and a pointed muzzle.*

❖ TEDDY LONG JOHN ❖

1905 "Last Bear of the Day" Steiff

Center seam typical of every 7th bear on the Steiff production line.

No trademark on left ear.

Nose restitched with black thread.

Large original black boot-button eyes.

Holes in original pads reveal that each footpad has different-colored felt underlay.

Pale cinnamon-colored mohair plush.

HEIGHT: 24IN (61CM).

A restorer recently discovered that this particular bear is stuffed with an ancient pair of long johns – a finding that supports the rumor that Steiff used to stuff its teddy bears with rags if the workers ran out of wood wool at the end of the day. The different-colored felt underlay on the bear's feet reinforces his "last bear of the day" status.

❧ MARMADUKE ❧
Pre-World War I British Teddy

Long blond mohair plush.

Large clear glass eyes with pink-painted backs and black pupils.

Distinct muzzle.

Nose stitching in green yarn – possibly the work of a repairer.

Replacement claws indicated with green yarn.

Body stuffed with wood wool and a growler that no longer works.

Large woven fabric pads on paws and feet.

HEIGHT: 16IN (41CM).

Although this bear carries no manufacturer's trademark, experts believe that he was made c.1913 by the British company, William J. Terry. This theory is based on an old photograph showing William J. Terry teddies for sale in Whiteleys, a London department store. Marmaduke strongly resembles the teddy bears depicted in the photograph.

❧ · WISTFUL · ❧
c.1907 Golden Mohair-Plush Bruin

Original brown glass eyes with black pupils.

Small rounded ears sit wide apart on head.

Left eye possibly a replacement.

Foxlike face with sharp, triangular muzzle.

Black thread stitches on nose are the work of a repairer.

Long curly golden mohair plush.

Long beige felt foot-pads.

HEIGHT: 13IN (33CM).

Wistful was made c.1907 by the Bruin Manufacturing Co. in New York. At the beginning of this century, many firms, such as the Harman Manufacturing Co., Columbia, and Aetna, were established in New York to meet the growing demand for Roosevelt-inspired toys. Like these companies, the Bruin Manufacturing Co. was short lived.

❧ WALTZING MATILDA ❧
1930s–40s Australian Joy Toys Bear

Golden yellow
mohair plush.

Nose
indicated with
vertical black
stitching.

Clear glass eyes
with amber-
painted backs and
black pupils.

Arms extend
the length of
the torso.

Unjointed neck –
a distinguishing
feature of many
Australian bears
of all ages.

Embroidered cotton
label bearing
manufacturer's
name stitched
onto beige felt
footpad.

Slightly
pointed,
upturned
paws.

HEIGHT: 15IN (38CM).

oy Toys was established by Mr. and Mrs. Kirby in South
Yarra, Victoria, Australia in the 1920s. It was one of the
earliest teddy bear makers in Australia (until the 1920s,
most had been imported from Great Britain and Germany),
but it was taken over by the British firm, Lines Bros., in the
1960s. The Joy Toys name was used until the 1970s.

❧ P.A. POOH ❧
1930s Top-Quality Chiltern Bear

High-quality, soft golden mohair plush.

Black vertically stitched nose.

Body-length arms shorter than those of German bears.

Replacement amber and black plastic eyes.

Velveteen pads – a distinctive feature of Chiltern bears.

HEIGHT: 20IN (51CM).

Made in the 1930s by H.G. Stone & Co. Ltd., P.A. Pooh is a fine example of a Chiltern soft toy. These were so-called because the toy-making factory was based in the Chiltern Hills of Buckinghamshire, England. With his big thighs and short arms, P.A. Pooh displays the key characteristics of a bear in the Hugmee range of bears.

❧ PARAMATTA PAUL ❧

Early Brown Mohair-Plush Steiff from Australia

Small black boot-button eyes.

Steiff button with raised lettering in left ear.

Typical pronounced muzzle.

Body stuffed with wood wool.

Feet have five claws; paws have only four.

Long limbs.

Worn brown mohair plush.

HEIGHT: 13IN (33CM).

Paramatta Paul, a small early Steiff, has spent most of his life in Australia. In 1903, an Australian sea captain bought him in Europe as a present for his daughter. The worn state of his mohair plush suggests that she loved the bear dearly. His present owners named him after his Australian hometown, Paramatta, just outside Sydney.

❧·CLAUS·❧
1927 Gebrüder Hermann Bear

Front of ear same material as muzzle.

Short-pile cream mohair plush on muzzle.

Brown glass eyes with black pupils.

Black horizontally stitched nose.

Dual-colored mohair plush – beige tipped with rich cinnamon.

Black thread claws stitched across mohair plush.

Small feet with oval cream felt pads.

HEIGHT: 17IN (43CM).

Stimulated by the teddy bear phenomenon, Johann Hermann founded a firm in 1907 to rival Steiff. Bears from the two German factories can be difficult to tell apart, although the muzzle of a Hermann bear is usually made from a different fabric than that on the head and body. Claus, a handsome teddy, was made by Gebrüder Hermann in 1927.

❧ BIG BEN ❧

Chad Valley's Typical British Bear of the 1940s

Large soft ears in excellent condition.

Large wide head.

Compact, vertical stitching on nose – a typical Chad Valley feature.

Original amber and black glass eyes.

Arms short compared to those of German bears.

Brown Rexine (oilcloth) pads on paws and feet. No claws indicated.

Good-quality golden mohair plush.

HEIGHT: 42IN (107CM).

Big Ben is the classic British bear. His big thighs, large wide head and ears, plump body, rather short arms, and rounded feet make him quite distinct from the German, French, and American bears of the same period (c.1940). His manufacturer, Chad Valley, whose factory was in Shropshire, England, was one of Merrythought's rivals at the time.

❧ AHSOO ❧

1930s Japanese Carnival Teddy Bear

Pinkish orange synthetic plush on knitted backing.

Large wired ears.

Velveteen muzzle with black stitched nose.

Original pink ribbon with bell tied at neck.

Arm joints connected by rod, so arms move together.

Stitched claws join up with painted claws on base of pads.

Short, stubby arms with unusually pointed paws.

HEIGHT: 15IN (38CM).

The distinctive painted claw patterns on Ahsoo's foot-pads, combined with the jointing system for his arms, suggest this bear has Japanese origins. Ahsoo is possibly a carnival bear, given as a prize at a fair. This particular example resembles Steiff's Teddy Baby – a bear cub distinguished by his exceptionally large feet and a bell around his neck.

❧· BING OH! ·❧

c.1911 Gebrüder Bing

Dark brown mohair plush.

Hand-embroidered triangular nose.

Mohair plush clipped around muzzle.

Large feet with replacement leather pads.

Original shiny black boot-button eyes.

Traditional inverted V-shaped mouth.

Metal button incised "GBN" under left arm.

Long arms and curved paws.

HEIGHT: 21IN (53CM).

This handsome brown bear, resembling Steiff bears of the same period, was a product of the German soft-toy manufacturers, Gebrüder Bing. In 1909, Steiff took legal action against this rival company to prevent them imitating the distinctive "button in ear" trademark. As a result, Bing Oh! bears a metal button trademark under his left arm.

❧ CHILI PEPPER ❧
1940s H.G. Stone & Co. Ltd.

Circular ears positioned wide apart and toward back of head.

Amber and black glass eyes.

Black hand-embroidered rectangular nose.

Characteristic down-turned mouth.

Large round muzzle occupies most of face.

Body filled with sub (cotton waste).

Musical mechanism contained in Chili Pepper's lower back.

Rayon typical of this period.

HEIGHT: 16IN (41CM).

This attractive coral-pink bear was made by a prominent British toy manufacturer based in the Chiltern Hills of England, and is subsequently known as a "Chiltern" bear. He is a musical teddy and plays "Brahms' Lullaby" when he is wound up. The clockwork musical mechanism is housed in Chili's lower back and is controlled by a protruding key.

❧ ARTHUR ❧

1930s Inexpensive Dutch Teddy Bear

Short-pile golden synthetic plush.

Enameled black and white metal buttons represent eyes.

Black vertically stitched nose.

Round, blunt, upturned muzzle.

Body tightly stuffed with wood wool.

Short, straight, slightly tapered arms.

Short-pile rayon plush on paw and footpads.

Absence of claws on paws and feet suggest that this was a cheap bear.

HEIGHT: 28IN (71CM).

Although Arthur van Gelden has no trademark, his strong resemblance to other Dutch bears, such as his heavy, compact stuffing, suggests that he was made in Holland. He belongs to an inexpensive line of large teddy bears, indicated by the absence of any claws on his paws and feet and the rayon plush that has been used for his fur.

❧ GIGI ❧
1930s High-Quality French Teddy Bear

Round black
boot-button eyes,
set close together.

Card label, bearing
manufacturer's
name, fastened
with metal button.

Cinnamon
vertical stitching
for nose.

Original white ribbon
tied in a bow.

Elegant, long,
slender body.

Faded pink rayon
in fairly good
condition.

Beige felt pads on
paws and feet.

Long, slim,
tapering legs.

HEIGHT: 17IN (43CM).

igi was made by Fadap, a toy-manufacturing company
founded in Divonne, France. Like Maurice, another
French bear (*see page 34*), she was made in the 1930s.
Gigi would have been more expensive than Maurice, because
she is made of quality materials and has a more sophisticated
jointing system (each arm and leg can move independently).

❧ BIG TEDDY ❧
c.1910 Kresge Family Bear

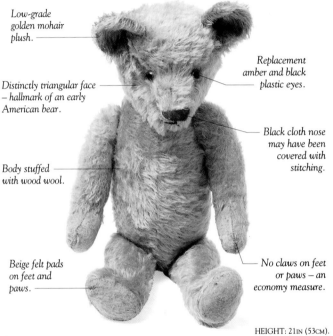

Low-grade golden mohair plush.

Distinctly triangular face – hallmark of an early American bear.

Body stuffed with wood wool.

Beige felt pads on feet and paws.

Replacement amber and black plastic eyes.

Black cloth nose may have been covered with stitching.

No claws on feet or paws – an economy measure.

HEIGHT: 21IN (53CM).

Many of the early American teddy bears did not carry a trademark, making their identification difficult. The fact that this teddy was made from cheap materials suggests that he is not an Ideal. Until recently, he had spent all of his life in the Kresge family, founders of the Kresge five-and-ten stores, which evolved into the Kmart chain.

❧· LINDY ·❧
Buck Hill Collection's First Steiff (1905)

Original black boot-button eyes.

Steiff button with raised lettering in left ear.

Black horizontally stitched nose.

Golden mohair plush in mint condition.

Body filled with wood-wool stuffing.

Four black stitches for claws on feet and paws.

Long, large, narrow feet.

HEIGHT: 12IN (31CM).

Lindy was the first traditional bear bought by Rosemary and Paul Volpp. Today, their Buck Hill collection, which numbers 5,000 bears, is considered the best in the world. The pattern from which this 1905 Steiff was made is similar to that of one of the earliest Steiffs put into production – the Richard Steiff bear that is held in the firm's archives.

❧· EDDIE ·❧
1903–1905 Blank-Buttoned Steiff

Small rounded ears placed wide apart – a feature of early Steiffs.

Blank nickel-plated Steiff button.

Black horizontal stitching on nose outlined by two diagonal stitches.

Small black boot-button eyes set close together.

Four paws, each indicated with a single black stitch across the mohair plush.

Replacement footpad.

HEIGHT: 13IN (33CM).

ddie is almost identical to Lindy (*see opposite*), except for the blank, nickel-plated button in his ear. Blank buttons were generally used between 1903 and 1905 before Steiff introduced their name on the button and prior to registering their "button in ear" trademark. These blank buttons were used occasionally after 1905 in order to use up old stock.

❧ STILL HOPE ❧
1907 Aetna Toy Animal Co.

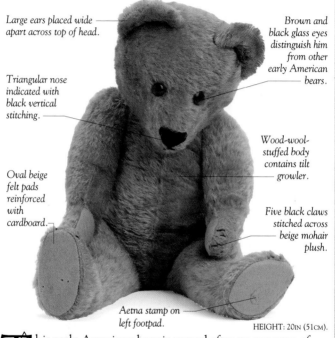

Large ears placed wide apart across top of head.

Brown and black glass eyes distinguish him from other early American bears.

Triangular nose indicated with black vertical stitching.

Wood-wool-stuffed body contains tilt growler.

Oval beige felt pads reinforced with cardboard.

Five black claws stitched across beige mohair plush.

Aetna stamp on left footpad.

HEIGHT: 20IN (51CM).

This early American bear is named after an ancestor of his present owners, who was scalped and left for dead. However, the ancestor recovered, and lived to reach the remarkable age of 110! Still Hope was made by the Aetna Toy Animal Co., one of the many American teddy bear manufacturers established in the early 1900s.

❧ CHUMMY ·❧
1930s Classic Merrythought Bear

Amber and
black glass
eyes.

Clipped mohair
plush on pointed
muzzle.

Body filled with
kapok and
wood-wool
mix.

Celluloid button
bearing firm's
name attached
to left ear.

Slightly shaggy golden
mohair plush.

Claw stitching on
paws typical of
Merrythought
bears of the
period.

Fabric label stitched
to right felt footpad.

HEIGHT: 23IN (58CM).

One of Merrythought's earliest creations, Chummy demonstrates the emergence of Britain's new-style teddy bear with shorter arms, a straight back, and a mix of kapok and wood-wool stuffing. These features distinguish him from the early German and American bears of this period, with their long limbs, hump backs, and wood-wool stuffing.

·❧ PERFECTION ·❧

c.1903 Prototype Steiff

Replacement
stitching on nose.

Shaved muzzle
very pronounced.

Head and limbs
jointed using
metal rods.

Black replacement
claws (original
stitching would
have been beige).

Elephant button
in left ear.

Original beige
stitching on
mouth just
visible.

Thick, curly white
mohair plush in good
condition with little
sign of wear.

Exceptionally long
arms extend
beyond legs.

HEIGHT: 15IN (38CM).

Steiff experimented with various prototypes to develop a
suitable pattern for production, so many early Steiff bears
differ slightly from one another. Perfection is probably one
of these prototypes, because she is unlike any known production
bears. White Steiffs are less common than golden or beige
Steiffs, but not as rare as the black models.

❧·M'LADY BRISCOE·❧
c.1940 J.K. Farnell

White mohair plush.

Head filled with wood wool.

Original amber and black glass eyes.

Short muzzle typical of British bears.

Limbs filled with kapok – a silky fiber from the seed pod of a tropical tree.

Printed Alpha Farnell label indicates c.1940 date.

Faded blue felt paw and footpads.

Absence of claws on paws.

HEIGHT: 13IN (33CM).

The Alpha series was a range of teddy bears patented by the London-based company, J.K. Farnell, in the 1920s. Kapok, the stuffing used for M'Lady Briscoe's limbs, was preferred by British firms because it is softer, lighter, and more hygienic than wood wool, and could be bought cheaply from countries within the British Empire.

❧ FRANCOIS ❧
French World War I Teddy Bear

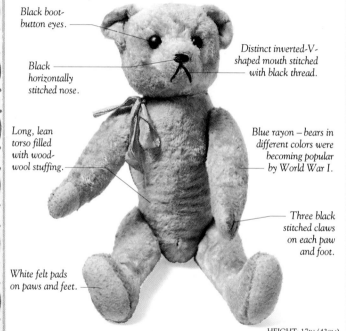

Black boot-button eyes.

Distinct inverted-V-shaped mouth stitched with black thread.

Black horizontally stitched nose.

Long, lean torso filled with wood-wool stuffing.

Blue rayon – bears in different colors were becoming popular by World War I.

Three black stitched claws on each paw and foot.

White felt pads on paws and feet.

HEIGHT: 17IN (43CM).

The first company to make teddy bears in France was Thiennot in 1919, when bans imposed on imports from Germany, the center of the toy-making industry, created opportunities for toy manufacturing to develop elsewhere. These bears are generally tall, elegant, and long-legged compared with their European and American cousins.

❦·DICKIE·❦
c.1950 German Schuco

Large brown glass eyes with black pupils.

Downturned paws – a feature of Schuco bears.

Body filled with kapok stuffing.

Rounded felt pads reinforced with cardboard.

Beige mohair plush, tinged with pink, in good condition.

Three long, black claws stitched across mohair plush.

Reverse side of original red plastic trademark reads, "Made in U.S. zone, Germany."

HEIGHT: 13IN (33CM).

Dickie's red plastic name tag indicates that he is a Tricky teddy – one of a line of Yes/No bears manufactured by the German firm, Schreyer and Co. (often abbreviated to Schuco). These bears all had small tails that acted as levers: by pulling the tail up and down and from side to side, the owner could make the bears nod or shake their heads.

❧ MR. ROOSEVELT SR. ❧
1940s New-Style American Bear

Golden mohair plush.

Large ears set wide apart – a feature of Knickerbocker bears.

Brown and black glass eyes, sewn into face seams, may be replacements.

Short, rounded, clipped mohair-plush muzzle.

Black vertical stitching for nose.

Short limbs less firmly stuffed with kapok than rest of body.

Beige velveteen pads.

HEIGHT: 20IN (51CM).

This teddy is the creation of the Knickerbocker Toy Co. Inc., a U.S. firm noted for the Smokey Bears it produced in the 1960s and 1970s. Although he was in fact made c.1940, Mr. Roosevelt Senior, with his large rounded head, flat muzzle, straight back, and short limbs, is more typical of the flatter teddy bears that dominated after World War II.

❧ LOUISE ❧
1921 White Mohair-Plush Steiff

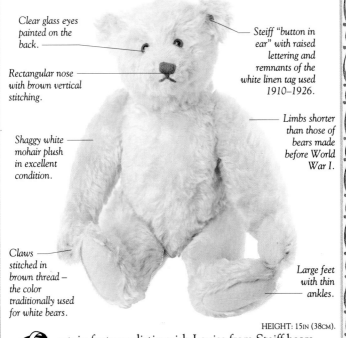

Clear glass eyes painted on the back.

Steiff "button in ear" with raised lettering and remnants of the white linen tag used 1910–1926.

Rectangular nose with brown vertical stitching.

Limbs shorter than those of bears made before World War I.

Shaggy white mohair plush in excellent condition.

Claws stitched in brown thread – the color traditionally used for white bears.

Large feet with thin ankles.

HEIGHT: 15IN (38CM).

ertain features distinguish Louise from Steiff bears made before World War I. She has glass instead of boot-button eyes, her limbs are shorter, and she is filled with a mixture of kapok and wood-wool stuffing to make her more cuddly. However, with her protruding muzzle and humped back, she retains the traditional Steiff bear shape.

⚜· GENTLE BEN ·⚜
Early U.S. Ideal Novelty & Toy Co. Bear (1904–1905)

Triangular face
– a feature of
early American
bears.

Small black
boot-button eyes.

Black
horizontally
stitched nose.

Five black
claws on
paws and feet.

Steiff metal
button added at
later date to
deceive buyers.

Beige mohair
plush in good
condition.

Feet slightly pointed.

HEIGHT: 11IN (28CM).

he Ideal Novelty & Toy Co. was the first firm in the
United States to make teddy bears. Gentle Ben, dating
from 1904–1905, is one of its earliest models. Ben's
pretty, distinctly triangular face indicates that he is an Ideal
bear, even though someone has sewn a Steiff button on his
left ear in an attempt to convince buyers otherwise.

❧ BRUNO ❧
Large 1909 Steiff

Large black boot-button eyes.

Steiff button with raised lettering in left ear.

Well-worn pointed muzzle.

Black thread nose with vertical stitching.

Beige mohair plush slightly worn.

Four black claws on each paw and foot stitched across mohair plush.

Hole in pad reveals felt underlay and wood-wool stuffing.

HEIGHT: 28IN (71CM).

Bruno, a large 1909 Steiff, arrived in the United States as padding around an English family's best set of china. As the demand for good-quality Steiffs increased, the English family decided to sell him to a dealer. His present owners, Paul and Rosemary Volpp, paid $4,000 for him in 1985 – a price that reflects his good condition.

❧ MR. FLUFFY ❧

1923 Chad Valley Bear with Aerolite Trademark

Small metal and celluloid button bearing Aerolite trademark.

Glass eyes held on wire shanks.

Long-pile golden mohair plush.

Black claws on paws and feet stitched across mohair plush.

Limbs filled with kapok stuffing.

Body, stuffed with kapok and wood wool, contains broken voice box.

Velveteen oval pads reinforced with stiff cardboard.

HEIGHT: 16IN (41CM).

had Valley, a company with a factory in Wellington in Shropshire, England, began specializing in stuffed toys in 1920 as demand for British bears grew. Manufactured in 1923, Mr. Fluffy was one of the company's first bears to carry the Aerolite trademark. Used between 1923–1926, the Aerolite name indicates that the bear was stuffed mainly with kapok.

❧ OTHELLO ❧
1912 Shaggy Black Steiff Bear

Large ears set wide apart and sewn into facial seams.

Black boot-button eyes, each set on an orange felt circle.

Long, shaggy black mohair plush.

Long, curved arms typical of early Steiff bears.

Steiff button with raised lettering in left ear.

Protruding, clipped mohair-plush muzzle.

Long, narrow pads of beige felt in perfect condition.

HEIGHT: 19IN (48CM).

Othello, a rare teddy bear, is one of only 494 shaggy black mohair teddy bears produced by Steiff for the British market in 1912. The German firm produced one other model of a black bear in 1907, but unlike Othello, he had red stitched claws, a sealing wax nose, and was without the distinctive orange felt circles that surround Othello's eyes.

❧ MAURICE ❧

French 1930s Depression Bear

Black boot-button eyes.

Slightly upturned, pointed muzzle.

Typical French profile – long and lean.

Original dark blue bow.

Metal joint disks attached to outside of arm and connected by a single rod.

Faded red cotton flannel instead of mohair or silk plush.

Blue cotton flannel pads on feet, but not paws.

Three black stitched claws on each foot and paw.

HEIGHT: 17IN (43CM).

This unfortunate French bear shows the tell-tale signs of having been made during the Depression. The absence of paw pads, the use of cotton flannel, his short limbs, and a jointing system that only allows the arms to move together (they usually move independently) all indicate that the manufacturer was economizing on materials and labor.

❧ MISS NIGHTINGALE ❧

c.1912 British Teddy Bear

Wide, high forehead is typical of British bears.

Small rounded ears gathered and fitted into seams of bear's face.

Unusual eyes made from round, convex pieces of metal painted black.

Wide smiling mouth made from black wool thread.

Arms shorter and straighter than her contemporaries.

Long, thin body and straight back.

Short-pile golden mohair plush.

Small, rounded feet with beige felt pads.

HEIGHT: 19IN (48CM).

One of the earliest of all British bears, Miss Nightingale is thought to pre-date World War I, dispelling the myth that the first bears are either German or American. She is unmarked, so unfortunately her makers are a mystery, but we can see how she differs from her German cousins with her long body, short arms, small feet, and straight back.

❧ BINGLE BILL ❧
Early 1920s Gebrüder Bing

Replacement brown plastic eyes with black pupils.

Pronounced muzzle of closely shaved mohair plush.

Black vertical stitching represents nose.

Long, silky, silver-tipped mohair plush, made specially for the teddy bear industry.

Orange button trademark on right arm.

Replacement beige felt pads.

HEIGHT: 23IN (58CM).

The orange button trademark, with the letters "BW" (Bing Werke) attached to this bear's right arm, confirms that he was made after 1919. Bing bears manufactured prior to this date carry a silver-colored button reading "GBN" (Gebrüder Bing Nuremberg) under the left arm. Bing bears are only rarely found with their buttons intact.

⁕·BERTIE·⁕
1930s British Teddy Bear

Large, triangular head with wide forehead.

Glass eyes, held on wire shanks, stitched into position.

Most of pile worn away on paw and footpads.

Wood-wool and kapok-stuffed body contains working tilt growler.

Stocky legs with large, stubby feet.

Worn label bearing manufacturer's name.

HEIGHT: 26IN (66CM).

In 1903, Henry Samuel Dean established Dean's Rag Book Co. in Fleet St., London. Originally manufacturers of rag books and printed cloth cut-out sheets of stuffed toys, they did not begin to produce plush teddy bears until the end of World War I. When Bertie was made in the 1930s, the company was at the height of its success.

37

⚜· BEAR OWNERS ·⚜

Dorling Kindersley would like to thank the following people, who generously lent their teddy bears for photography:

• Heather Bischoff
for Marmaduke page 7

• Gyles Brandreth,
from the Teddy Bear Museum at Stratford-upon-Avon in the UK, for Claus page 12

• Pauline Cockrill
for Chili Pepper page 16

• Pam Hebbs
for Eddie page 21 and Louise page 29

• Ian Pout
for Othello page 33

• Private Collection
for Arthur page 17

• Judy Sparrow,
from The Bear Museum at Petersfield in Hampshire in the UK for Chummy page 23; Mr. Fluffy page 32 and 39; Miss Nightingale page 35 and Bertie page 37

• Paul and Rosemary Volpp
for Teddy Long John page 1 and 6; Gentle Ben page 1 and 30; Lindy page 2 and 20; Bruno page 3, 4 and 31; Dickie page 5 (top) and 27; Wistful page 5 (bottom) and 8; Waltzing Matilda page 9; P.A. Pooh page 10; Paramatta Paul page 11; Big Ben page 13; Ahsoo page 14; Bing Oh! page 15; Gigi page 18; Big Teddy page 19; Still Hope page 22; Perfection page 24; M'Lady Briscoe page 25; Francois page 26; Mr. Roosevelt Sr. page 28; Maurice page 34; Bingle Bill page 36 and 41; and the replica of Happy page 38.

❧· USEFUL ADDRESSES ·❧

MUSEUMS

Bethnal Green Museum of Childhood
Cambridge Heath Road
London E2 9PA, England
☎ (081) 981-1711/6789

Franny's Teddy Bear Museum
2511 Pine Ridge Road
Naples, Florida 33942
☎ (813) 598-2711

Good Bears of the World
2352 Valeway Drive
Toledo, Ohio 43613

Margaret Woodbury Strong Museum
1 Manhattan Square
Rochester, New York 14607
☎ (716) 263-2700

The Steiff Museum
Margarete Steiff GmbH
PO Box 1560
Alliin Straase 2
D-7928 Giengen (Brenz)
Germany
☎ (49) 7322-1311

MAGAZINES

Hugglets Teddy Bear Magazine
Glenn Jackman
PO Box 290
Brighton BN2 1DR
England
☎ (0273) 697-974

The Teddy Bear and Friends
Hobby House Press
900 Frederick Street
Cumberland, Maryland 21502
☎ (301) 759-3770

Teddy Bear Review
Collector Communications Corp.
PO Box 1239
Hanover, Pennsylvania 17331
☎ (717) 633-7333

❧· INDEX ·❧

⚜·ACKNOWLEDGMENTS·⚜

Dorling Kindersley would like to thank the following photographers for their contributions to this book: Jim Coit 1, 2, 3, 4, 5 (top and bottom), 6, 8, 9, 10, 11, 13, 14, 15, 18, 19, 20, 22, 24, 25, 26, 27, 28, 30, 31, 34, 36, 38, 41; Roland Kemp 7, 12, 16, 17, 21, 23, 29, 32, 33, 35, 37, 39.

We would also like to thank the following for their help: Susan Thompson for editorial help; Ann Terrell and Sam Grimmer for design assistance; Alastair Wardle and Peter Howlett for their DTP expertise; and Michael Allaby for the index. Our special thanks go to Paul and Rosemary Volpp for their patience and generous contributions to the book.

Border illustrations by Pauline Bayne.
Illustrated letters by Gillie Newman.